0

DOING MORE WITH LESS

A Guide to the Size Zero Enterprise

By Philip Letts

SIZE
ZERO

Published by blur Group, 2015

Eagle House, 1 Babbage Way,

Exeter Science Park, Exeter, Devon

EX5 2FN   +44 (0) 1392 927 182

blurgroup.com

Printed by Create Space, Amazon

This little book aims to tell a big story.

It's about the silent revolution of Size Zero Business which is infiltrating management strategy in boardrooms from Seattle to Sydney, reshaping the very core of commerce.

If you haven't heard about it, then I guess this is your moment.

I will confess right now that I am not an economist, an academic, a management guru or a prophet. I am just a businessman with something to say.

Philip Letts

ABOUT THE AUTHOR

Philip has run a string of high profile web ventures across the US and Europe including an established Silicon Valley venture.

In 1998, he co-founded internet currency business beenz.com which was valued at $300 million just two years later.

In 2000, he became CEO of the business trading exchange Tradaq, before moving to lead the mobile technology start-up Surfkitchen which was later sold to Symphony Teleca.

In 2006 he set up blur which has since grown into the world's largest online marketplace for business services.

Philip's blur Group now processes millions of dollars of business between marketing, legal, IT and accountancy service providers and commissioning clients.

blur Group, which has offices in Exeter, London and Dallas is listed on the London Stock Exchange's AIM Market.

CONTENTS

INTRODUCTION

Over the past year, I have sensed that something important is going on out there in the world of business. Something is stirring. However you want to describe it, you can be sure of one thing: it's going to change the rules of the game, perhaps for ever.

Here's what I think is happening: the river of technological progress which has swept most of us off our feet over the past decade has hit the slower flowing waters of economic recession. And just as in the real world, my metaphorical rivers have created a swirling caldron of uncertainty and opportunity.

To be fair, technology has always given us the means to achieve great things, but until now there's been no real pressure to embrace it. The global down-turn has changed all that. Where there was a way, there is now a will.

We are witnessing the rise of slimmer, smarter businesses that operate in new ways, taking advantage of new collaborative technologies and a globally available resource base.

These organisations are 'just big enough', highly

focused on delivering value, and use data to drive insights and innovation. Some of these businesses were start-ups not that long ago and some are long-established organizations, but all share a new mindset and belief that growth does not mean the number of people you have in your organization, but the value you create.

I like to think of these organizations as Size Zero Enterprises.

Size Zero means operating at maximum efficiency by focusing on where value is created, and being ruthless in removing waste. Doing more, with less if you like.

An example of a Size Zero big Enterprise is Amazon who realised from inception that the value of a retail business was not in its stores, but in its ability to manage inventory, not all of it within its own facilities, and built a global retail giant with no physical stores. As a result, Amazon's revenue per employee hit $855,000 last year compared to a store-based operation like Gap which managed a mere $108,403.

It is important to state that a Size Zero business is not about slashing headcount - it is much full time employee *(The 10 Principles of Open Business, David Cushman and Jamie Burke).*

There is another compelling reason why outside resources should be embraced. Statistically, the bigger your company gets the more average it will become. To counterbalance this unfortunate side effect of growth, new thinking from outside service providers can be invaluable.

While many organizations have for years used some combination of in-house work and outsourcing (no computer company makes its own furniture, grows the wheat for bread in the employee cafeteria, or makes waste paper baskets), where should the line be drawn? How does the company decide what to buy, and what to produce? The answer is: value. The Size Zero organization decides which approach, at every stage, costs less, improves quality, or in some other way increases value for itself, its customers, its brand, or the environment.

Size Zero is not about downsizing, it's about re-shaping to create more value. Slimmer, smarter, faster - not smaller.

Technology clearly has a huge impact on efficiency and productivity, but few companies invest enough in R&D. The US is pretty smart when it comes to R&D, investing some 2.79% of GDP. But with just 1.7% of GDP spent on research, the UK lags well behind the rest of Europe.

One big ticket item not allowed in a Size Zero

Enterprise is overtly expensive office space which can account for around 10% of the cost line. In most cases, this property is a burden not an asset. It's no surprise that the short term rental and shared workspace business is booming when companies are faced with crippling rents and taxes that add no value to anyone.

In the digital age with cloud computing and ubiquitous communication, location is largely irrelevant and there are bargains to be had by moving out of your comfort zone. Or better still, how about sending your workforce home?

Twelve months ago, blur relocated from its London premises and moved 200 miles west to Exeter. The company saved around $240,000 on property costs and the staff found their salaries went a lot further in the local economy. blur itself is now on the journey to become truly Size Zero with every job, task or project being posted on to the marketplace. It has grown revenues year on year with zero increase in headcount.

The rules of business, fashioned centuries ago during the industrial revolution, are there to be broken.

The "we've always done it like that" culture is being eroded by technology, globalisation and the super-slim businesses it has helped create.

Making radical changes to the way your business operates isn't going to happen overnight, but it does start with a commitment to change.

ZERO INEFFICIENCY

It's getting harder to spot a successful business. A couple of decades ago we could tell from the company car park and the size of the pension fund, but today the number of employees is no longer a valued metric for success.

Take a look at the electric car company Tesla which has turned out 50,000 vehicles since opening its first factory in California in 2003. Tesla employs only 6,000 people yet the company has a market cap of $34 billion. Compare that with GM which has a market cap of $155 billion, yet has a staggering 205,000 people on its books.

The value of Tesla all comes down to its revenue per

employee ratio which is overall revenue divided by the number of employees.

The latest figures show Tesla delivering a mind blowing $2.7m per employee, whilst GM could only achieve $750,000.

Clearly, Tesla has been able to achieve more with less which is the cornerstone of the Size Zero Enterprise.

The company puts its productivity down to a number of factors but mainly that it has kept employee numbers down by relying on outside suppliers and assembly automation.

The company's Model S sedan has at least 26 different suppliers providing parts which leaves Tesla itself with an assembly only role - much of which is done by robots. It's a fact that most high performing companies do not manufacture their own products. For example, all Apple's iPhone and iPad products are manufactured by Foxconn of Taiwan who employ a staggering 1.2 million people but can only dream of hitting Apple's margins who employ just 80,000 people but have similar revenues at around $150bn.

So, we've learned that the most successful companies have high earnings per employee ratios and they achieve that through automation and outsourcing.

Another good example of how disruptive thinking can generate a valuable business is Ryanair.

Now, many of us love to hate this budget airline because of its hard-line attitudes toward customer service, but the business is undeniably sound.

Their strategy was Size Zero from day one.

- Only operate one type of aircraft to keep maintenance costs down and to attract discounts on bulk orders.

- Based on the fact the aircraft only make money when flying, minimise time on the ground with quick turn-round times achieved through discouraging hold baggage.

- Keep costs down by choosing less popular airports some way away from the major cities.

- Automate the booking process through the website

- Create additional income from add-ons for reserved seating, bag check in and refreshments. This practice netted them $338million in Q1 of 2014 alone.

Despite a bit of blip last year, Ryanair is back on track and delivering a whopping $560,000 per employee which is a sector leading figure.

The other key driver of uber efficiency in business is outsourcing and the big question is which functions to outsource and which to keep in house. It's a topic that draws a lot of debate, but that's not surprising as it's largely responsible for the transformation of the United States from a manufacturing to a service economy.

However, what interests us about outsourcing is not so much the physical redistribution of labour, but the intellectual one.

Where do good ideas come from? Well, it's rarely from within.

Not because payrolled staff don't have the creative talent, but because proximity to a problem can reduce one's ability to find a solution. You can't see the wood for the trees.

Accenture recently researched this area and discovered the majority of innovation is created by service providers or a joint effort between the client and the supplier. Only 17% of innovation came from within.

At blur, we have a 1 in 10 rule. Only one in every ten people working on our business is working in our business. By adopting this policy, we have effectively increased the brainpower of the business 100 fold. In a business like ours intellectual capital is everything, so idea farming is a key part of our business strategy.

Of course, outsourcing has now given birth to a disruptive child nurtured by the internet - crowdsourcing. This is outsourcing on a huge scale to unspecified suppliers and tends to be more outcome focussed than outsourcing. It's a technique getting mainstream adoption across the globe including from international brands like Pepsi and Coca Cola which are turning to their millions of Facebook followers to help with marketing and product development.

As the world slowly emerges from global recession it is incumbent on everyone in business to shape up for the new opportunities that lie ahead.

If automating a business process can release vital cash for growth - do it. If sourcing talent from outside the company can give you an injection of innovation - do it.

THINGS TO DO TODAY

1   Work out your revenue per head (revenue divided by number of employees) and use it as a barometer for the fitness of your business. Look at the figures achieved by the best in your sector and set them as your benchmark.

2   Consider how far you can go with outsourcing, and start referring to it as "rightsourcing"- a useful term which will help keep the sceptics at bay!

3   Talk to your board about introducing the one in ten headcount rule. If my experience is anything to go by, you will find it both productive and liberating to have more people outside your organisation than inside it.

4   Don't be the last business to join the crowdsourcing party. My company, blur, was built on the principles of crowdsourcing and after nearly a decade in business we are still only skimming the surface of this brilliant way of optimising brainpower.

5   Automate as much as you can. Robots are good people, really!

ZERO PASSENGERS

Do you have passengers in your business? People who turn up for work but don't actually seem to accomplish much? If so, your business is far from unique.

The reasons why people fail to live up to their full potential at work are many and varied. Low morale, whether work-related or not, can hit productivity. Inefficient business processes can reduce output. Lack of skills or training can prevent workers from delivering their best.

Whatever the reason, passengers cost you money and contribute little to your bottom line. And if it's not your business that's holding them back, you might want to think twice about keeping them on.

In the past it may have been OK for some people to coast along within the corporate structure, but there is no room for passengers in today's Size Zero Enterprises. As McKinsey puts it, "a business is a value delivery system."

If your people are not part of that value chain, they shouldn't be part of your business.

The wisdom of ditching such passengers is clear, but it's something very few companies currently do. Partly that's to do with HR concerns or the financial hit of a redundancy package for long-standing yet inefficient staffers. Higher up the corporate ladder, political considerations come into play. You can't let go of Bill, for instance; he used to be the senior partner.

Furthermore, despite the recent financial crisis there are still lingering concerns over getting the right staff. Last November Fortune reported that Silicon Valley companies were hiring 'perks managers' to keep employees happy… and loyal.

But war-on-talent worries miss the point that any talent that isn't helping your business perhaps isn't worth fighting for.

So how do you move towards having zero passengers? The first step is to have a clear idea of what you mean by 'value'. It might not always equal money. For a web business, for example, having an ace digital architect on board might be critical for success. Similarly, the top negotiator in your customer claims department is clearly adding value even if they are not personally bringing in cash.

Once you've established your top-tier value makers, check to make sure there aren't good reasons why some of your other people aren't performing. Are there signoff bottlenecks stopping them from being productive, for instance? Have they been given the right level of responsibility? Are they fully aware of company goals?

When you have checked that these and other factors are not holding people back then the chances are you will have a list of employees whose contribution to the business might be less than clear.

With these you might want to apply some final, common sense tests for value. Have they recently made a significant contribution to the business, for example?

Does anyone notice when they go on holiday?

Are they part of a critical support structure for others who do offer great value?

If the answer to these questions is 'no' then they probably wouldn't get a job at a company like Tesla.

And if you aspire to be a size-zero business then maybe they shouldn't be working at yours.

'Zero passengers' means operating a business where everyone adds value.

Where every team is an A team. Every worker is an office hero. And every line on the payroll is a guaranteed investment in growth.

The benefits of a zero-passenger policy are not just financial. Being strict with passengers will leave you with a higher-functioning, more highly efficient business that will be more competitive. And ironically, letting go of poorly performing people could boost staff morale when those left realise they are part of a higher-everyone pulls their weight. So far so good. But what happens when you need to take on more people? Even the best screening process in the world can't prevent the odd passenger from getting through. The answer is simple: don't hire.

At blur, our one-in-ten rule means only 10% of the people who work for us actually draw a salary.

The rest of our work is outsourced to specialists around the world. They pitch for each project, in the same way as they would for one of our customer's projects, and so have to prove their value from day one. And they all get paid on results, giving them the ultimate incentive to perform.

Callous? Hardly. The sellers on our platform are all seasoned professionals who relish their independence and their ability to pick and choose the work they do best. They only pitch for projects where they know they can add value and they take personal responsibility for getting it right.

If you adopt this approach your business gets the maximum value from the people who work for you, in a completely transparent and equitable way.

And if you really feel you have to take people on then go down the Google route. The company is so hard to get into that there are even books about its recruitment process. But you can bet the people who do get in are pulling their weight.

THINGS TO DO TODAY

1   The first step to maximizing people power is to work out what "adding value" means in your business. Think about life without each and every one of your team (including yourself). Would your customers suffer?

2   Make sure that your business is not holding back your people. Are you making it difficult for them to do their jobs?

3   Once you've identified the passengers, act quickly but fairly. The sooner they get off the bus, the better for everyone.

4   Review your recruitment policy and don't automatically leap for the payroll option every time there is a need to hire.

5   Being payrolled can sometimes engender complacency, so, once again, look at my one in 10 rule where 90% of human resource is sub contracted.

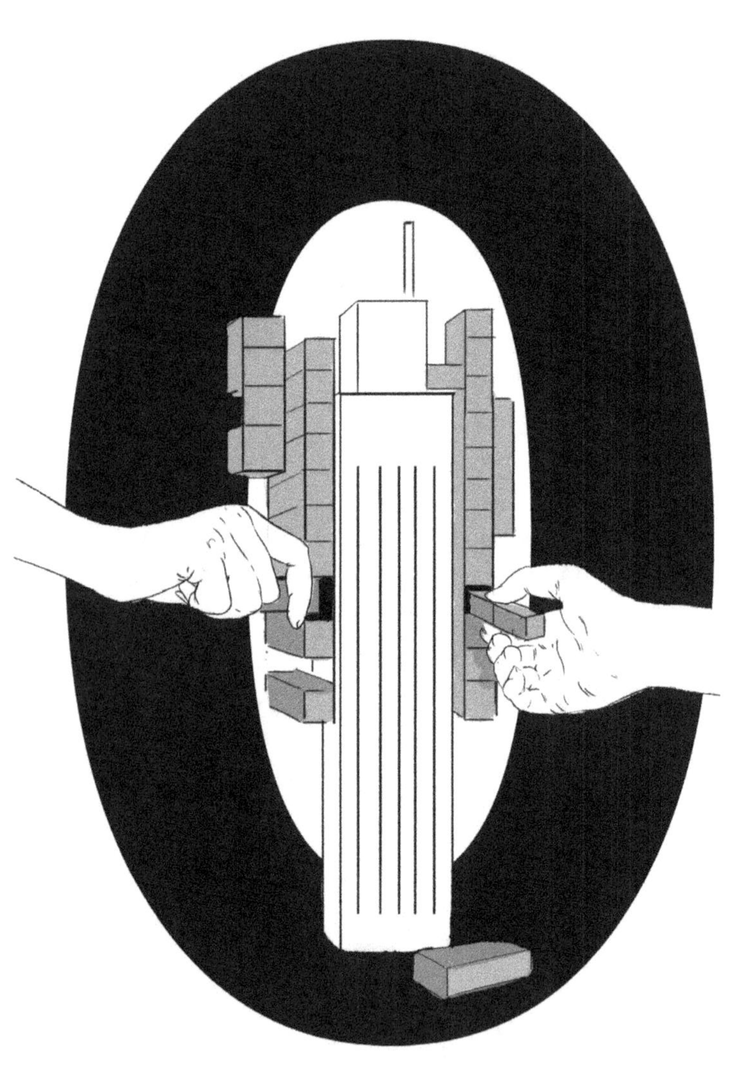

ZERO BAGGAGE

"If you wish to travel far and fast, travel light", said Cesare Pavese. He was a poet, but the quote would hold good for many of today's business leaders.

For some time now, businesses have been aware that it hardly makes sense to do everything yourself. The age where every single business function was carried out in-house is now long gone.

Instead, non-core processes such as payroll management or IT service desk provision are now routinely outsourced. The benefits are clear. Your company saves on employment costs and you can adjust the scale of your outsourced services to meet the vagaries of business growth. End of story? Not quite.

While outsourcing is practiced frequently, it is rarely used to its full extent. Few companies have gone to the extreme seen with Nike, for example. The sportswear giant made nearly $28 billion last year by marketing over 500,000 products made by more than a million factory workers. But it only has 56,500 employees, giving it a revenue per head of $495,000.

How about your business?

Are you certain everything you're doing at the moment couldn't be done better and cheaper by anyone else? Really?

A new generation of enterprise leaders is showing that these days you can pretty much build a business on the basis of a good idea… and little else. Whatever more you need, you just buy in. A couple of years ago Carol Roth, author of The Entrepreneur Equation, posted a blog entry listing no fewer than 75 tasks that your business could outsource.

Of course, there's a risk involved in farming stuff out. But given the ease with which you can now outsource projects, and the range of suppliers you can choose from, it is almost fairer to say you run a risk of getting left behind if you don't outsource.

In particular, it's worth bearing in mind that outsourcing doesn't just give you access to more (and potentially much cheaper) talent, but also opens the door to new purchasing models. Besides fixed-price, time-and-materials and cost-plus deals, in sectors such as IT you can now take advantage of gain-sharing, incentive-based, consumption-based and shared risk-reward pricing schemes, for instance.

All of these can help you keep a tighter rein on cash flow and ultimately improve the competitiveness of your business.

Outsourcing in itself is not the cure for all ills, though. If your supplier networks are going to act as a true extension of your own business then you have to pay as much attention to quality and process factors as you would within your own company.

A tendency to 'outsource and forget' is perhaps what has led to some disillusionment in recent years, and something of a reversal in the outsourcing trend. Sometimes functions have been taken back in house, but the smarter response has been switch to 'rightsourcing', defined as choosing the correct source for a service based on cost, quality and expediency.

As part of any rightsourcing analysis, it's worth asking whether you have all the right supplier relationships in place to begin with.

Let's say you are getting poor value from an international

marketing agency. Maybe you could switch agencies. Maybe you could take the work in house. But if your business is only focused on a couple of different markets, maybe you could just outsource the work to in-country professionals who would do a better job than an agency, at lower cost.

In a similar vein, while having supplier rosters is often a handy way of cutting procurement admin, be aware that inflexible roster systems can hamper your ability to find the best talent at the best price. If the aim of a roster is to simplify paperwork, then maybe your best bet is to simply work with a multi-vendor services platform that offers standardised purchasing, invoicing and payment.

And if you want to take outsourcing to its ultimate conclusion, try crowdsourcing: getting the expertise or resources you need not from traditional suppliers, but larger groups such as online communities. With crowdsourcing, the scale of talent you can access is almost limitless, allowing you to meet the needs of just about any project and any budget.

The bottom line for a Size Zero Enterprise should be not just to make sure you can focus efficiently on your core business but try crowdsourcing: getting the expertise or resources you need not from traditional suppliers, but larger groups such as online communities. With crowdsourcing, the scale of talent you can access is almost limitless, allowing you to meet the needs of just about any project and any budget.

The bottom line for a Size Zero enterprise should be not just to make sure you can focus efficiently on your core business but that every in-house and supply chain function is delivering the maximum value.

In striving to achieve zero baggage, you need to ditch old-fashioned ideas such as 'growth equals headcount' or 'company versus supplier'.

Instead, look at your business as an ecosystem within which you deploy the best combination of resources available, in-house or externally, to meet the demands of your customers. You need to rip up your linear org chart and redraw it to include all the other human resources engaged with your business. Now alone will you see the true reach of your business - actually around 10 times bigger than you imagined - but it will become very clear where efficiency gains can be made.

When blur created its new style org chart (fig.1), we saw our organisation in a new light. We were no longer a small team sitting in an office in Exeter, but a network of thousands of people all over the world, each able to contribute real value to the business.

Adopting a flexible, mix-n-match approach to business processes can yield results like you wouldn't believe. Going back to Nike, in 2009 the brand with the swoosh decided it needed to focus more on social media. It switched its athlete endorsement programme, the cornerstone of its marketing, away from TV stars and onto sports champions with big Facebook and Twitter fan bases.

The move not only put Nike in touch with a younger, hipper, social-media savvy audience… but also cut the company's sponsorship bill by around $400 million in a year.

THINGS TO DO TODAY

1 Ask yourself whether everything you do couldn't be done better and cheaper by someone else. You will be surprised by the answer!

2 Look at your business in a holistic way, seeing your suppliers as much a part of your team as the people on your payroll. It will bring a very helpful perspective to your HR management.

3 Don't just think of outsourcing the unsexy side of business. Some of the best results come from outsourcing the idea generation process. Many brains make light work of innovation.

4 Make sure your organization is not the last one in the world to try crowdsourcing. Put the challenge out to your people or even your customers.

5 Think of your talent pool as a talent ocean. And remember, you may have to cross a real ocean to find someone who's right for your organization.

(fig.1) We are blur Group

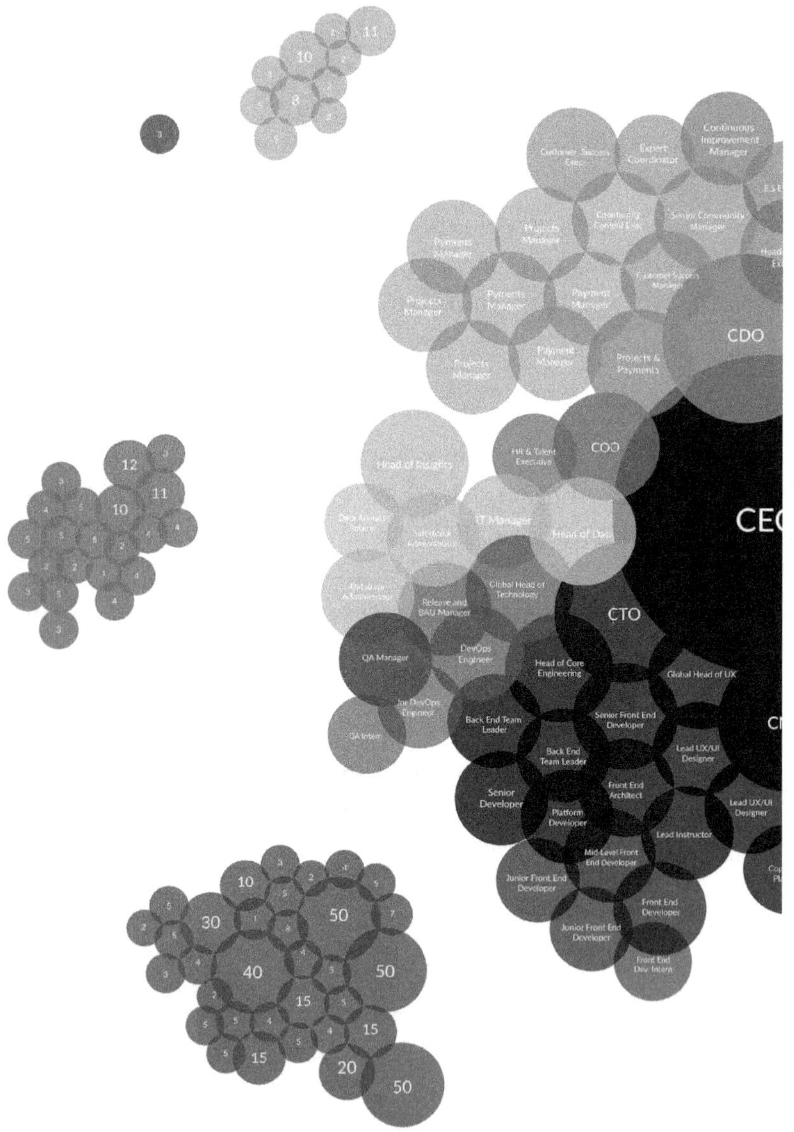

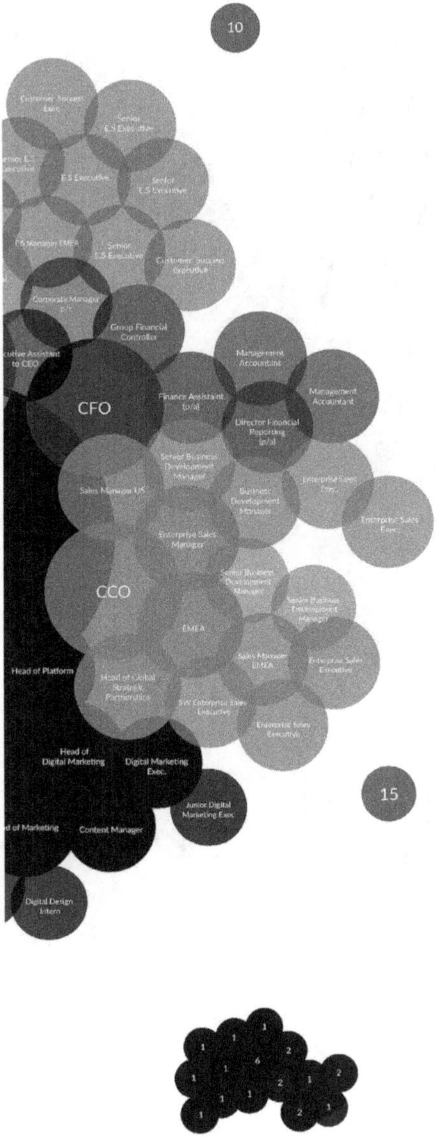

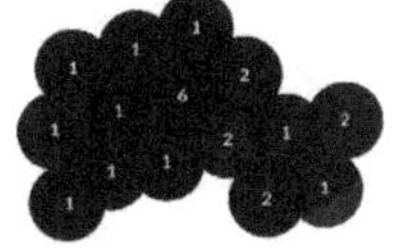

We have 60 full-time employees

**672 Service Provider employees
work on our business**

We use 106 services:

19 of which for Finance
25 of which for Technology
14 of which for Marketing
22 of which for People Ops
6 of which for Community
4 of which for all staff

$0

ZERO PROPERTY COSTS

Dick Whittington famously said London's streets were paved with gold. Today it's not so much the streets as the office space that's worth a fortune. According to CBRE Research's Global Prime Office Occupancy Costs survey, the UK capital is the most expensive place on earth for you to have offices. Prices are almost $274 a square foot in London's West End.

Hong Kong is not far behind, at $251 psf, while in Beijing and Moscow you can expect to pay up to $198 and $165 psf, respectively. Perhaps surprisingly, you'll even get stung for office space in India. A corporate outpost on Connaught Place, New Delhi, will set you back by almost $159 psf. If you're intending to run a size zero enterprise then you really want to think twice about shouldering this kind of burden.

After all, technology nowadays lets you hop onto video calls with your customers and partners wherever they are in the world (and can save travel costs no matter where you are). For rare in-person meetings, you can grab a low-cost flight to almost anywhere for less than a train fare. Paying through the nose for exclusive office space just doesn't add up.

Even in averagely priced areas, office space can account for a tenth of your costs. And each square foot carries further hidden expenses in the form of maintenance, security, insurance and so on. What can you do about it? More than you would think, perhaps.

Here are nine ways a size zero enterprise could knock a zero or so off property costs.

1. Move to a cheaper area.

Move to a cheaper area. It sounds obvious, but seriously: how much added value do you get from being in a high-cost city such as London? At blur, we were able to save $240,000 just by leaving the capital for Exeter, 150 miles away. Our staff found their wages went further, too.

Even among the world's 50 priciest property markets

there is enough variation for you to make major savings. In Leeds, UK, for example, you only pay a quarter of London West End prices.

2. Get people to work from home.
If you can't move completely then the next best option is to occupy less space. And to do that you can simply tell staff to stop coming into the office.

Home working is nothing new. Back in the year 2000 the telecommunications giant BT told 10% of its staff, or 10,000 workers, to stay at home. Thanks to home working, BT now saves around $960 million a year. But today the trick is not so much to send workers home as to recruit home workers in the first place, for instance in the form of freelancers or short-contract staff.

3. Outsource parts of your business.
Outsourcing has a number of potential advantages, but one big plus in high-rent areas is that you no longer have to find office space for workers.

4. Find other ways to cut the size of your office.
If you can't move out any more staff, what about other stuff? Old-fashioned IT server rooms, for example: why not put all your systems in the cloud? Can you digitise documents and other media, to free up libraries? Use smarter stock-keeping practices to minimise storeroom space?

5. Investigate serviced premises.

Serviced office providers are usually presented as a premium accommodation option but the degree of competition in the market has reduced prices. And if you have very specific space requirements, renting serviced offices by the square foot may work out better than having to take a gamble on a larger space that you may not grow to fill. The ease of administration and flexibility in rental terms are other advantages to bear in mind.

6. Sub-let your premises.

If you can't move out, get someone else to move in. See if you can rent unused office space to third parties and ease the strain on your bottom line. Bringing in other businesses is not just financially smart, but if you choose your office partners carefully you could benefit from cross-fertilisation of ideas and a richer work environment.

7. Rent what others won't touch.

If you really have to stay in a high-price area, think whether you really need premium office space. Don't forget that the popularity of loft-style offices came about because at one point they were much cheaper to rent. Today, loft space is hardly cheap. But you may find other types of accommodation that are.

8. Play with timing.

Although the key to property is 'location, location, location', timing can also play a part. Take a leaf out of the pop-up store playbook and ask yourself whether you can take advantage of short-term or transient opportunities to reduce costs and maximise your real estate spend.

And the killer? Do all of the above. After all, size zero isn't about following rules.

It's about doing whatever it takes to increase the value of the business.

Whatever office environment that may be in.

THINGS TO DO TODAY

1   Remember that thinking outside the box will often end in working outside that box you call your office.

2   Work out what would happen to your margins if you had no property costs whatsoever. Clearly, not achievable, but it will reveal the scale of the opportunity.

3   Think the unthinkable and work out what you'd save by renting the ugliest building on the block and the most unfashionable side of town.

4   Remove all the private offices in your building. You will create desk space for at least four more people and it would force your senior managers out on the floor where they should really be.

5   Squeeze your landlord (not literally). Outrageous demands have a habit of being met whilst little requests are easily ignored.

PROJECT

ZERO UNPROFITABLE CUSTOMERS

You know about the 80-20 rule? The one that says 80% of your profits come from just 20% of your customers? What are you doing about it? In many organisations, the answer is probably 'nothing'.

Traditional businesses tend to see customer numbers as a key performance metric. So they don't care if a customer is contributing a lot or a little to the bottom line.

But for companies that aspire to be size zero enterprises, with high profits, low costs and great customer service, the 80-20 rule is vitally important. Or to put it another way: it's important to have zero unprofitable customers.

Admittedly it's not easy. You may have more unprofitable customers than you think. In one case reported in Forbes, a family business with 1,100 customers found that 350 of them weren't contributing to the bottom line. Quite the opposite: the company was losing $2 million a year by servicing them.

Another example is the insurance firm Marsh & McLennan, which politely asked thousands of customers to leave in 2005 after discovering that 25% of its client base was unprofitable.

Hanging onto unprofitable customers is not just going to hurt your balance sheet. It's also going to damage your reputation with the customers that do keep you afloat.

The reason is simple. In most cases, customers are unprofitable because they demand more of your services than they pay for. That means other customers that do pay more are getting less of a service than they deserve.

So what can you do with unprofitable customers? The obvious answer is to let them go. But the process has to be handled delicately so as not to upset your other customers, or the employees who have invested time and effort in building loss-making relationships.

According to Forbes, four things you should not do with unprofitable customers are to introduce across-the-board price hikes (because you may hurt profitable business), selectively allocate costs, confuse profit with revenue… or get emotional. Dealing with unprofitable business is purely a business decision.

Nor should you be shy of making tough decisions when you need to. The Harvard Business Review says 90% of executives interviewed in 2005 and 2006 had thought about divesting customers and 85% had actually gone ahead with it.

Once you have said goodbye to your unprofitable customers, it's time to renew your focus on the most profitable ones.

This process starts at the customer acquisition phase. The Oregon-based IT managed services provider Convergence Networks, for example, is said to have boosted revenues by 9% in 2013 after turning away 90% of new business opportunities and simply focusing on the four new customers worth most.

Convergence is not some fly-by-night operation. It's a $7 million business with a 97.5% customer satisfaction rating, listed among Oregon's top 100 employers and top 100 growth companies. And when it comes to unprofitable customers, it's clearly a size zero enterprise. Don't you think your business should be operating in a similar way?

THINGS TO DO TODAY

1 Reassess. Find out not just which customers are unprofitable, but why. Have they been left behind in a change in company focus, for example? Are they simply on the wrong products, plans or programmes? Could a few simple measures make them profitable for your business?

2 Educate. If customers require a lot of servicing it may be because they are suffering from a knowledge gap regarding your products. Check to see if your manuals, training and so on are up to scratch. Make sure you set the right expectations in your sales process. Promote automated helpdesk services and self-service channels.

3 Renegotiate. In many cases it may be worth speaking to your customers about paying more for the unprofitable services they use. To do this, you need to clearly articulate your value proposition and show why it makes sense for the customer to pay extra. Importantly, having this conversation

helps to set the scene if you need to take things to the next stage.

4 Migrate. For customers where renegotiation is not going to work, you can take matters into your own hands and shift them onto a lower service level. This could mean moving them onto a self-service channel, for example, or delegating the relationship to junior or outsourced staff. Another option is to refer the customers to a business partner that is better set up to take on the work, perhaps in exchange for a small finders' fee.

5 Terminate. If all else fails then it makes sense to end the relationship. The critical thing is to use tact and diplomacy so you avoid negative fallout. Make sure you communicate the decision well in advance and where possible attempt the other measures outlined above beforehand.

ZERO TECHNOPHOBIA

RadioShack's collapse has got to be one of the most poignant stories in recent corporate history. The company that helped introduce technology to the masses for almost a century went bust after failing to adapt to a new technological landscape.

Press accounts of what went wrong at the retail chain speak of employees playing video games to pass the time, in stores where a customer wouldn't be seen for hours on end. Those that did show up often went away disappointed, as they were looking for advice that RadioShack's low-paid and poorly trained staff were unable to give.

Most importantly, though, RadioShack fell behind in a world where you can buy almost anything online and get it delivered to your home. "RadioShack's executives never committed to e-commerce," Canada's Financial Post reported, "in part because they were worried about diverting attention from the difficulties at the stores."

It's a shame because RadioShack's core business of selling electronics components to hobbyists seems tailor-made for online success. Then again, nowadays just about anything can be a success online.

Companies such as Amazon and Google have not just become synonymous with internet success but have also been the driving force behind a new generation of tools that make it easy for everyone to go digital.

Amazon Web Services, for example, gives you reliable, scalable and inexpensive cloud computing capacity, doing away with the need for you to invest in costly data centre infrastructure. Google, meanwhile, offers a range of business email, communication and collaboration tools within its Apps for Work suite.

I know what you're thinking at this point: these web-based offerings are all well and good for people who want to cut corners without worrying about quality. But they're not for serious businesses, right?

Wrong. Companies using Amazon Web Services include Dow Jones, Pfizer and NASA. And 5 million businesses use Google Apps for Work, including Hewlett-Packard, PricewaterhouseCoopers and Whirlpool.

In fact, with mainstream business applications such as the Microsoft Office Suite now being offered via the cloud, too, it really makes little sense to pay extra for the hardware and maintenance you need to run anything in-house.

Adopt a size zero enterprise mentality regarding technology and the savings you can achieve are staggering.

Take a function such as marketing, for example.

Instead of buying or building an enterprise customer relationship management system, you can use Salesforce.com from the cloud with prices starting at $65 per user a month. Rather than pay for an in-house web development team for your corporate communications web pages, you can copy The New Yorker, BBC America or Sony Music and use WordPress. And in place of costly content distribution systems or customer surveys you can employ a cheap or free service such as MailChimp and SurveyMonkey to keep in touch with customers and get their feedback.

Judicious use of such low-cost services could easily

shave a zero or two off your marketing budget, with no appreciable impact on the quality of your operations.

Quite the opposite: unlike an in-house system, services such as Salesforce.com or WordPress are built to cater for millions of users, so they are less likely to crash or suffer security glitches. The companies that provide these services take care of updating them and adding new features, so you don't have to. And in most cases these technology tools are childishly simple to use, so your people don't have to take time off for costly training.

Looking for additional savings? Well, cloud-delivered applications are just the start. Instead of wiring up your office and installing desktop PCs, why not just throw up a Wi-Fi network and give all your workers a tablet computer that they can use for everything from accessing corporate applications to videoconferencing, wherever they are?

Then take a look at your processes and ask if some of them could be handled by technology instead of people.

Can you cut the cost of customer acquisition through self-service automation, for example? Slash administration time by running expenses claims through a web-based system such as Concur? Use smart video surveillance systems to reduce your physical security overhead?

By the time you have reached this point you should be well on the way to the zero-technophobia ethos characteristic of Size Zero Enterprises. But what about the expertise needed to manage your technology estate? If you are no longer managing large amounts of hardware and software in-house then you don't need a large IT team. On the contrary, you can cut your IT department to the bone and hire people on a temporary basis as and when the need for skills arises.

Bear in mind that you can now access talented technology experts around the globe, for anything from application coding to research and development consulting, often at a fraction of the price that it would cost you to have them on payroll. Provided there's a network connection you can find the right person for almost any job, at the right price.

Technology is more than ever the key to cutting costs and boosting profits.

RadioShack failed to get that message, but if you are looking for size zero then you need to be in tune with zero technophobia today.

THINGS TO DO TODAY

1 Take your head out of the sand and stick it in the cloud. It's where computing is done nowadays and I can't think of a reason why anyone would prefer a bank of servers in the stationery room.

2 If you are not already doing so, start using those wonderful cloud services like Mailchimp, WordPress, salesforce.com and Survey Monkey.

3 Don't reprimand the digital generation for doing digital things like social media. It's part of their DNA which you should be exploiting, not suppressing.

4 Appoint an AO – an automation officer whose job it is to come up with plans to automate everything. Seriously, you will never know how far you can go until you have been over the edge.

5 Make that technology investment everyone has been nagging you about.

ZERO BUDGETS

You would think that anyone working for a company with 'Texas' in its name would be conditioned to think big. But when it came to budgeting, Texas Instruments manager Peter Pyhrr did the opposite. He thought zero. "Each year he prepared his budgets as if last year's figures had not existed," recounts The Economist. "Every assumption had to be rethought from scratch and then justified."

This was back in the 1960s.

Pyhrr described his process in a 1973 book called Zero-based Budgeting: A Practical Management Tool for Evaluating Expenses.

There was brief interest in the method, with Jimmy Carter even going so far as to propose it as a way of cutting US federal budgets in his 1976 presidential campaign.

But in those days before office computers many people were put off by the large numbers of calculations involved.

Fast-forward four decades and computing is no problem. On the other hand, 'budget bloat' is. Basing next year's expenditure on what you spent this year is not exactly an efficient way of controlling costs. In particular, sales, general and administrative costs have a habit of growing year on year until they start to outpace growth in revenues.

So for companies seeking a smarter, sleeker, Size Zero Enterprise way of doing business, Pyhrr's zero-based budgeting is back in fashion.

Investopedia defines zero-based budgeting as: "A method of budgeting in which all expenses must be justified for each new period" and notes that it "can lower costs by avoiding blanket increases or decreases to a prior period's budget."

How much lower? McKinsey & Company tells of a company that saved 11% of its operating budget within four months of introducing zero-based budgeting.

The company reinvested 40% of the savings back into customer-facing staff.

More generally, McKinsey says zero-based budgeting can typically lop between 10% and 25% off sales, general and administrative costs, "often within as little as six months."

The consultancy also demolishes some common myths that have grown up around zero-based budgeting. It's not simply a way of building budgets from zero, for example; it's a repeatable process that can create a sustainable culture of cost management.

Nor does it always imply doing away with all costs. In reality, the degree of cost reduction can be set by the company strategy and so is up to the requirements of the business in a given point in time.

Another myth is that even with computing support a zero-based budgeting exercise will be so time-consuming that everyday business will ground to a halt.

Nobody argues that zero-based budgeting is more onerous than simply rolling an existing budget from one year to another. But in practice it can be achieved by a single central team, led by the finance and IT functions, in four to 10 months. To get the hang of it, McKinsey recommends starting with a pilot scheme across a single business function.

One other misconception is that zero-based budgeting only applies to sales, general and administrative costs. Not so: it can be applied to just about anything, with minor adjustments.

Finally, some people believe zero-based budgeting is not intended for companies that are growing aggressively. This too is false. In fact, it's a good way to cut out unproductive costs so money can be spent in more useful areas.

If zero-based budgeting sounds like a lot of work, then it's worth remembering that it is basically for people who are really serious about making money.

One company that regularly uses the practice is a Brazilian private equity firm called 3G, led by Jorge Paulo Lemann, the richest man in Brazil. Since buying Burger King in 2010, 3G has tripled the fast-food chain's profit margin, to 61%.

And in 2013, when 3G teamed up with Warren Buffett's Berkshire Hathaway investment house to buy Heinz, the ketchup maker was taken back to basics in a zero-budgeting exercise aimed at saving $150 million. Last year 3G repeated the stunt with Tim Hortons, a Canada-based doughnut chain. "The Canadian company can expect to get lean. Really lean," reported Bloomberg.

Recently there have even been calls to apply zero-based budgeting to cut the world's biggest budget: Obama's $4 trillion US government spending package. If Americans want an administration that's as efficient as a Size Zero Enterprise, the proposal deserves some serious consideration.

THINGS TO DO TODAY

1 Carry out a reality check of what you really need in order to complete your strategic objectives in the next budgeting period. Then give yourself a cost target.

2 Work out how much you are currently spending, where, and on what.

3 Map out what you need ideally to achieve your strategy.

4 Use a bottom-up approach to create that ideal state and the activities it requires.

5 Assign new budgets and full-time employee levels to the new state.

DELIVERY

ZERO STOCK

I have been pushing the idea of the size zero enterprise as something of a novelty. But some parts of it, at least, have been around for decades. Look at Toyota: the Japanese auto giant has been managing to achieve almost zero stock levels since the 1950s.

Today Toyota's celebrated just-in-time manufacturing practices are still a major feature of the business.

Says Toyota: "'Just-in-time' means making 'only what is needed, when it is needed, and in the amount needed.'

"For example, to efficiently produce a large number of automobiles, which can consist of around 30,000 parts, it is necessary to create a detailed production plan that includes parts procurement.

Supplying 'what is needed, when it is needed, and in the amount needed' according to this production plan can eliminate waste, inconsistencies and unreasonable requirements, resulting in improved productivity."

Although Toyota has made just-in-time manufacturing its own, the company freely admits it didn't come up with the notion. "The idea behind it was borrowed from supermarkets," says the firm. "A supermarket stocks the items needed by its customers when they are needed in the quantity needed, and has all of these items available for sale at any given time."

Dell, the computer maker, pretty much built its business on the practice of just-in-time and achieved notably short lead times for product delivery by getting suppliers to carry most of its inventory.

Harley Davidson, meanwhile, applied just-in-time principles in its progression from a World War II-style motorbike manufacturer to an iconic brand that is competitive in the 21st Century. Just-in-time manufacturing helped the company cut inventory levels by 75%, while boosting productivity.

These and other examples show how reducing stock to the bare minimum is a simple yet highly effective way to control costs.

To put it another way, every minute that a product or component is left sitting on a shelf it is costing you money.

In an ideal world, you would conjure up products from thin air just as your customer was handing over the cash to buy them. What happens if you snap your fingers and nothing appears, though?

The danger of supply chain failures has been cited as just-in-time's major weakness. Relying on deliveries with split-second precision could be dangerous if the delivery boy can't make it, the thinking goes. However, real-life experience seems to show just-in-time practices make companies more resistant to supply chain problems, rather than less.

It appears that because just-in-time manufacturers have to pay special attention to their supply chains, they tend to be more aware of potential problems and more likely to have a contingency plan in place. Dell, which had dispensed with warehouses altogether by 2004, provides a good example.

In 2002 analysts got ready to write the company off when strike action closed 29 shipping ports along the US West Coast. As it happened, however, the company had already been monitoring the likelihood of strikes and had commandeered 18 Jumbo Jets to fly components in from Asia. "In the end, Dell did the impossible," reported Fast Company. "It survived a 10-day supply-chain blackout with roughly 72 hours of inventory, and it never delayed a customer order."

Clearly, then, it pays for manufacturers to adopt just-in-time practices. But what if you're not a manufacturer? Here is where we at blur propose a further size zero Enterprise twist. In the knowledge economy, your human talent is pretty much your stock. And that, too, can be procured on a just-in-time basis.

On the blur platform, for example, you can source experts or teams for just about any knowledge-based task in just a few hours. Contract terms and payment are all agreed upfront and you do not even need to worry about billing, since it's all taken care of through blur's platform. Recent projects have ranged from a $2,500 luxury goods concept brief to the creation of a $300,000 global marketing strategy.

As with just-in-time manufacturing, zero stock processes applied to human resources can greatly improve corporate efficiency and reduce costs.

You avoid the expenses associated with recruitment, employment, training, sick leave, holidays… anything, in fact, not directly associated with getting the job done on time and to budget.

Zero stock also allows you to be more nimble as a business. Need to launch a new product? Set your budget, write the brief and get developers, legal experts, marketing teams and the rest bidding on your project tomorrow. By next week you could be signing off concepts and by next month you might be seeing a return on your investment, without having had to hire a single full-time employee.

That kind of flexibility isn't just good for your business. It's good for your health. With zero stock, your organisation should run more efficiently, which means less stress and more time to do important things like test drive your next company car. This time round, you might want to think about a Toyota.

THINGS TO DO TODAY

1   Don't ignore lean business just because you are not in manufacturing like Toyota. Even people-based enterprises like lawyers and accountants can reap the benefits of lean thinking.

2   Read Lean Thinking, by Womack and Dan Jones.

3   Consider introducing just-in-time stocking principles in your business, even if it's just for stationery.

4   Apply the Zero Stock rule to human resources. Don't allow people to sit around waiting for work. Create a talent tap using external suppliers, which you can turn on and off.

5   Get in contact with blur www.blurgoup.com to help with your just-in-time resourcing.

ZERO WASTE

You know sustainability is a big deal when a hard-nosed businessman like Paul Polman, Unilever's chief executive, starts going on about it. In a recent talk that must have raised eyebrows among investors, Polman struck out at business leaders who put profits ahead of sustainability. "If you make closed-loop systems you de-risk your model and it's good for the planet," he said.

By 'closed-loop', Polman meant 'zero waste'. Sustainability and profit "don't need to compromise," he said. As purveyors of the size zero enterprise, we wholeheartedly agree. In fact, we'd go a step further: if you are wasting anything then your business clearly isn't as efficient as it could be. And that's likely costing you money. Polman knows this.

Unilever's investment in zero-waste manufacturing helped the company increase its profits by 7% last year even though revenues were down.

How far can you go in terms of achieving zero waste? Michael Braungart and William McDonough claim you can go all the way. Noting that in nature everything eventually gets recycled, in 2002 the sustainability thought leadership duo published Cradle to Cradle: Remaking the Way We Make Things, a zero-waste manifesto. "Imagine a world in which all the things we make, use and consume provide nutrition for nature and industry," says McDonough, "a world in which growth is good and human activity generates a delightful, restorative ecological footprint."

Notably, the two environmentalists take issue with the prevailing reduce, reuse and recycle approach to sustainability. Instead they argue for manufacturing processes that involve upcycling: converting waste material into new or improved materials or products. In cradle-to-cradle thinking, the objective is to make sure every one of your products ends up either as technical nutrients, which can be reused for industrial processes, or biological nutrients, which can be released safely into the environment.

This is truly innovative thinking. Most of today's businesses are only concerned with getting products to market, selling them and potentially offering some kind of after-sales service. What happens at the end of that process is largely irrelevant.

With cradle-to-cradle, all business processes start with the question: where does my product end up? This may sound like an onerous way to go about things, but if you can re-use half of your old products to make new ones then you've just saved 50% on your materials costs.

How achievable is this vision? Perhaps more than you would think. Climatex Lifecycle, a furniture upholstery fabric manufacturer, makes zero-waste products from wool and ramie, a form of nettle. Its trimmings get used as gardening mulch. Honeywell and Shaw, meanwhile, have eliminated the need to send worn-out carpets to landfill by creating a process to make new carpet materials from old ones.

For an increasing number of enlightened business leaders, such a rethink of industrial processes is not just desirable but necessary.

The Global Footprint Network warns: "Today humanity uses the equivalent of 1.5 planets to provide the resources we use and absorb our waste. This means it now takes the Earth one year and six months to regenerate what we use in a year. Moderate UN scenarios suggest that if current population and consumption trends continue, by the 2030s, we will need the equivalent of two Earths to support us. And of course, we only have one."

From a big-picture perspective, striving for zero waste is simply a market investment.

Without sustainability, there may one day be no commercial markets left to exploit.

More immediately, though, it is a simple way to identify and cut costs. Doug Morrow, vice president of research at Corporate Knights, which runs a global corporate sustainability ranking, says: "It means doing more with less; squeezing more output out of every capital input, including financial, human and natural capital." It's also a potential competitive differentiator. Nielsen's 2014 Global Survey on Corporate Social Responsibility found 55% of global online customers in 60 countries would be happy to pay more for "for products and services from companies that are committed to positive social and environmental impact."

THINGS TO DO TODAY

1   If you don't have one already then think about taking on a chief sustainability officer or similar strategy leader (and remember you don't necessarily need to have them on staff).

2   Start looking for zero-waste quick wins that will add rapid value to your business.

3   Tackle your carbon footprint. Besides doing a lot of good for your corporate image, aiming for zero carbon can bring about almost instant reductions in energy and travel costs.

4   Manage your tailspend - the 20% or so of corporate purchases that do not go through your standard procurement channels. Since nobody usually controls these purchases, they potentially represent poor value for money. Worse still, they could be a risk to your business if they involve suppliers that do not adhere to your supply chain guidelines.

5   By imposing a blanket zero waste policy you can gain a measure of control over these costs and risks… and start seeing immediate benefits for the planet and for your business.

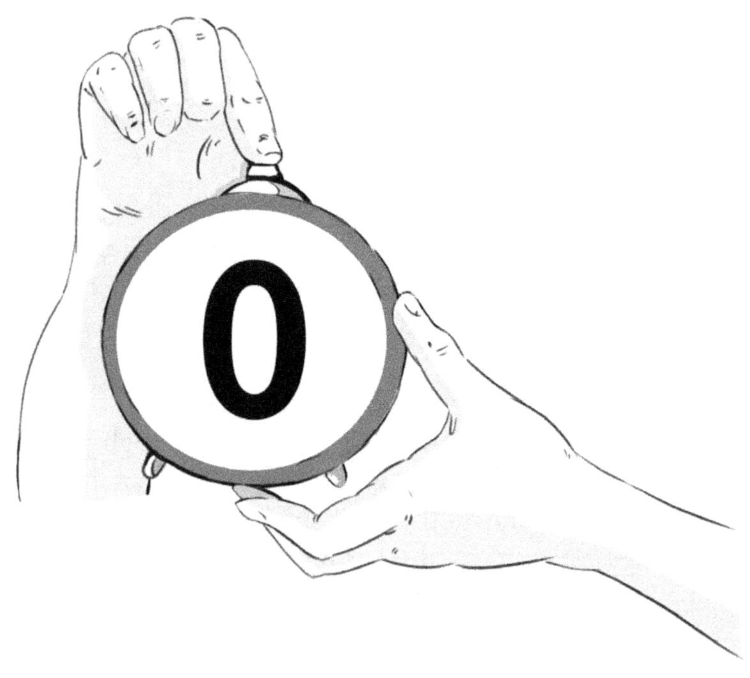
0

ZERO DEAD-TIME

Back in the day you needed to have a really good reason to invite Andy Grove to a meeting. The former Intel boss once wrote: "Just as you would not permit a fellow employee to steal a piece of office equipment, you shouldn't let anyone walk away with the time of his fellow managers."

Treating timewasters on a par with thieves may sound a bit harsh, but if you think about it such an attitude could well be justified. After all, you are paying your people to be productive. If someone or something is holding them back then you are losing money. And the drain is probably a lot greater than you think.

A study last year by the consulting firm Bain & Company estimated that about 15% of an organization's collective time is spent in meetings. The amount has been rising every year since 2008. And about 20% of that time is unproductive, equating to a whopping $60 million loss for a company with 10,000 employees.

Corporate meetings are incredible time vampires.

Bain uncovered one company with a weekly leadership meeting that added up to 7,000 hours a year for the attendees, but 300,000 hours a year for the workers who had to prepare materials for it.

The enterprise software company Atlassian, meanwhile, says workers today have an average of 62 meetings a month. About 50% of these end up being a waste of time, representing about 31 unproductive hours a month per employee.

Because meetings are so often useless, workers no longer take them seriously.

The cost? A whopping $37 billion, says Atlassian. In the US alone. But that's not all. When not stuck in pointless meetings, your people are likely to be swamped with useless emails. A busy executive can get

200 emails a day, or 30,000 a year. Even an average of around 300 a week, though, can be a serious drain on resources.

Bain's research, meanwhile, uncovered 22% of meeting participants sending at least one email per 10 minutes of meeting time, on average, and double-booking meetings to put off decisions about which to attend. "Dysfunctional behaviours like these create a vicious circle," says the Harvard Business Review. "Parallel processing and double booking limit the effectiveness of meeting time, so the organisation sets up more meetings to get the work done."

Apart from the time spend checking for and dealing with emails, Atlassian says the strain of constantly fielding messages can literally make you stupid. You can lose up to 10 IQ points, the same as missing an entire night's sleep.

Finally, there's the cost of interruptions at work: phones ringing, people dropping by for a chat and that irresistible urge to see what the office wag has sent to your cubicle neighbour. Workers say 80% of these interruptions are trivial.

With all this, it's a wonder any work gets done at all in a modern office.

In fact, Atlassian estimates that only about 60% of your time at work is actually productive. That's a sobering thought. It means at least 40% of your payroll spend is a complete waste.

THINGS TO DO TODAY

1. Create a zero-based time budget. Do to time what your finance department should be doing to expenditure. Decide in advance how much time your people should spend in meetings, give it to them as a fixed budget for them to spend, and include penalties for anyone who goes over. Start looking for zero-waste quick wins that will add rapid value to your business.

2. Consider why people waste time. It's because they are being paid for an input: their time. They have no incentive to become more productive. Pay people for output, instead, and the picture changes.

3. Cut all meetings in half. Do you really need a full hour? Give everyone just 30 minutes and watch productivity soar. Another tip: re-appraise who is needed. If someone is not going to add value to the meeting, they shouldn't be there.

4   Ramp up your spam filter. Spam costs $1,250 per employee in lost productivity. While you're dealing with it, educate people about sending pointless emails, too. They cost a further $1,800 per employee.

5   Send your people on a writing course. Poorly written communications cost up to an additional $4,100 per worker. Show your people how to get to the point and save time.

CONCLUSION

When I started down the road to Size Zero, it seemed like a lonely path. I meet with some fairly hostile reactions along the way and at the time I questioned whether I was being too radical and too idealistic. But as the months went past, I meet other people who shared my views and other enterprises already practising what I was preaching. Perversely, I get much comfort from the fact that I did not invent Size Zero Business, but merely coined the term.

In years to come, I will look back on this book and think of it as a statement of the obvious.

It will be the way business is practised by the majority of enterprises across the globe. Of course there will be exceptions, particularly with high-value, hand-crafted products and highly customised personal services, but I am not sure commerce will survive unless it gets fitter and slimmer.

I am often asked whether robots are the ultimate expression of Size Zero. Whether man will eventually be replaced by a more efficient version of itself? It is a scary thought but the signs are that the science fiction is becoming science fact.

Carl Benedikt Frey, an economist, and Michael A.

Osborne, an associate professor of machine learning, at the University of Oxford predict that over the next 20 years, the US will lose 50% of its workforce to automation.

Their gloomy forecast is based on some pretty sound criteria. Computing power is doubling every 18 months, machines are getting smarter and humans getting ever more canny in their search for the uber-efficient business model. It's already started to happen. Big Enterprises like IBM and Coca Cola are taking the grim reaper's scythe to jobs on a colossal scale in the face of tough trading conditions and the introduction of new technologies.

Volunteering will be huge with massive social enterprises formed to tackle issues like poverty and crime. The State will re-assert itself as a wealth creator, heavily taxing the hugely profitable automated businesses to fund education and social enterprise.

A new class system may evolve: a true working class and a new thinking class whose work-less world will be filled with learning and solving social and environmental issues. The thinking class will be paid through state grants based on societal contribution.

Perhaps a form of apartheid will return as tension between the two classes grows. Workers-only bars will emerge, open only to those with good old fashioned jobs. The thinkers will form an intelligent underclass meeting in private clubs…

Ok, I may have been carried away on an Orwellian flight of fancy here, but the fact remains that change is now a permanent feature of business life.

Of course, the death of work has been greatly exaggerated but I do believe that for every two jobs lost, at least one new one will be found.

ACKNOWLEGEMENTS

I would like to thank a number of friends and colleagues who helped clarify my thinking, research ideas and produce this little book.

Nick Band for sharing his views on the future of business.

Jason Deign for his tireless help with research.

Petra Zhivkova for her terrific illustrations.